my favorite animal

Bighorn Sheep

I0895071

Published in the United States of America by Cherry Lake Publishing
Ann Arbor, Michigan
www.cherrylakepublishing.com

Reading Adviser: Marla Conn MS, Ed., Literacy specialist, Read-Ability, Inc.
Book Design: Jennifer Wahi
Illustrator: Jeff Bane

Photo Credits: © Ian Maton / Shutterstock.com, 5; © sumikophoto / Shutterstock.com, 7; © Lorraine Logan / Shutterstock.com, 9; © Steve Boice / Shutterstock.com, 11; © Warren Metcalf / Shutterstock.com, 13, 21; © Tom Reichner / Shutterstock.com, 15; © Wildnerdpix / Shutterstock.com, 17; © Laura Cleasby / Shutterstock.com, 19; © Andrew Sabai / Shutterstock.com, 23; © Ozerina Anna 2-3, 24; Cover, 1, 8, 12, 20, Jeff Bane

Library of Congress Cataloging-in-Publication data on file

Printed in the United States of America
Corporate Graphics

table of contents

Looks 4
Home 10
Food 14
Habits 18
Glossary 24
Index 24

About the author: Dr. Virginia Loh-Hagan is an author, university professor, former classroom teacher, and curriculum designer. Her husband met a bighorn sheep when he climbed a mountain. She lives in San Diego with her very tall husband and very naughty dogs. To learn more about her, visit www.virginialoh.com.

About the illustrator: Jeff Bane and his two business partners own a studio along the American River in Folsom, California, home of the 1849 Gold Rush. When Jeff's not sketching or illustrating for clients, he's either swimming or kayaking in the river to relax.

looks

Bighorn sheep have thick horns. The horns curl. Males are **rams**. Females are **ewes**. Rams have bigger horns.

These sheep can weigh 300 pounds (136 kilograms). They can be brown. They can be gray. They have a white bottom.

They have **hooves**. Their hooves are like rubber. They hold tight to the ground. This helps them move and climb.

home

These sheep live in North America. There are three types. One is from the Rocky Mountains. One is from California. One is from the desert.

They live in mountains. They like rocky areas. They can't move in deep snow. So they move to valleys in winter.

These sheep **graze**. They eat plants. They eat grass. They eat seeds. They eat in the mornings. They nap in the afternoons.

Their stomach has four parts. They eat. The food comes back up. They chew it again. This is called chewing their cud.

They are social. They live in herds. Most herds have about 10 sheep. But a herd can have more than 100 sheep. Rams live apart from ewes.

Rams have **butting** contests. They hit heads. Their horns crack.

Rams fight for ewes. They join herds with ewes to have babies. Ewes give birth on high cliffs. They do this to protect their babies.

glossary & index

glossary

butting (BUHT-ing) ramming heads

ewes (YOOZ) female bighorn sheep

graze (GRAZE) to feed on land covered by grass or other plants

hooves (HOOVZ) the hard parts that cover the feet of animals

rams (RAMZ) male bighorn sheep

index

babies, 22–23
butting, 20–21

color, 6

eating, 14–17
ewes, 4, 18, 22

herds, 18
home, 10–12
hooves, 8
horns, 4–5, 20–21

rams, 4, 18, 22

size, 6